Fruitcake Recipe Cookbook

Delightful Non Alcoholic Fruitcakes for Holidays And Beyond

A M JACOB

Table Of Content

Wishing you peace and joy this holiday season and throughout the coming year.

Laura & Sherra

BigPictureCoaching.net

Introduction

Greetings from the magical realm of "The Fruitcake Recipe Cookbook." You will learn how to make mouthwatering fruitcakes that will be the talk of the party in the pages of this culinary adventure. Fruitcakes are a treasured custom all across the world, especially during the Christmas season, and have a rich and lengthy history that dates back centuries.

Your guide to discovering the rich and varied world of fruitcakes is this cookbook. There are many recipes and baking techniques available to suit every taste and ability level, regardless of your degree of experience. You may discover the ideal fruitcake for every occasion, ranging from traditional recipes that arouse memories of previous holidays to contemporary versions that introduce novel and inventive tastes.

As you scroll through this book, you'll come across numerous fruitcake recipes and acquire a thorough understanding of the supplies, equipment, and techniques required to make these delectable works of art. You will discover the techniques for creating fruitcakes that are juicy, aromatic, and loaded with a variety of nuts, fruits, and spices.

However, this book is not merely a compilation of recipes. It's a recipe book for creating visually stunning and delectable fruitcakes. You will explore the art of fruitcake decorating and presentation, learning tricks and methods that will turn these delicious treats into gorgeous focal points for your events.

Each dish comes with comprehensive step-by-step directions, ingredient lists, and practical advice to help you succeed in the kitchen. You can make fruitcakes for a family get-together, a holiday, a beloved custom, or just to nosh on a lazy afternoon; "The Fruitcake Recipe Cookbook" offers all the recipes you need.

So welcome to the world of fruitcakes, both with your heart and your kitchen. As you set out on a delightful journey, let the perfume of blended fruits, spices, and nostalgia permeate your house. A true labor of love and a sign of warmth and celebration, fruitcakes made with the help of this cookbook can be baked for yourself, your loved ones, or just the delight of giving.

Prepare yourself for a voyage that honors the art of baking as a culinary craft, as well as the delight of sharing special moments with loved ones and enjoying life's little pleasures. Together, let's embark on an exciting journey into the world of fruitcakes and turn every bite into a delicious memory.

"

Holidays are about creating cherished memories with loved ones and finding magic in the simplest moments.

JEREMIAH SAY

GRACIOUSQUOTES.COM

Chapter 1:

What Is Fruitcake?

Fruitcake is a sweet, thick confection with a distinct texture and nuanced flavor. It is usually distinguished by the blend of nuts, spices, and dried and candied fruits. Although it can be enjoyed all year round, this traditional cake is frequently connected to festivals and special occasions like Christmas and weddings.

Fruitcakes are known for their unique texture, which varies from moist and dense to somewhat crumbly. The high concentration of components, such as fruits and nuts, gives the cake a pleasing chewiness and contributes to its solidity. These components work together to create a balanced blend of sweet, nutty, and spicy aromas that give fruitcake its rich flavor. The addition of spices like allspice, nutmeg, and cinnamon gives the dish a deeper, more hearty quality.

Fruits and Nuts: The main ingredients of fruitcake include candied fruits like orange peel, cherries, and raisins, as well as dried fruits like dates, currants, and raisins. These ingredients add a chewy, fruity character along with little bursts of natural sweetness. Nuts like walnuts, pecans, and almonds give the cake a rich, nutty flavor and a gratifying crunch. One of the characteristics that makes fruitcake unique is the mix of nuts and fruits.

Cultural Significance: Fruitcakes are associated with many different cultures and traditions. For instance, many countries appreciate the Christmas fruitcake tradition, but different versions, such as the German Stollen and the Italian Panforte, are treasured in their own cultures. Fruitcakes are a common celebratory food, representing wealth, luck, and the sharing of memorable occasions.

Versatility: Fruitcakes are adaptable and can be made to accommodate a range of dietary needs and tastes. A diverse spectrum of individuals can relish them thanks to variants such as vegan fruitcakes, gluten-free choices, and light fruitcakes. Furthermore, fruitcakes can be artistically adorned and presented in a variety of ways, such as cake slices, cookies, bars, or even muffins.

Fruitcake is a dessert that combines nuts, spices, and dried and candied fruits to create a distinctive flavor and texture combination. Even though it's frequently connected to holiday customs, this treat is great all year round. It is still a favorite dessert for many due to its cultural significance and adaptability, and it represents celebration and community.

A Synopsis of Fruitcake's History

A quick look into fruitcake history reveals a varied and rich journey spanning continents and decades. Fruitcakes have a colorful history, and their development reflects shifting gastronomic customs and cross-cultural blending. Without getting into the essential components or geographical differences, we'll only talk about the historical turning points of fruitcakes here.

Early Beginnings: Fruitcakes have historical roots in prehistoric societies. Bread stuffed with nuts and fruits and sweetened with honey was a common dessert in ancient Egypt. Despite having a simpler composition, these early fruitcakes provided dependable and transportable energy for lengthy travels.

Medieval Europe: During the Middle Ages, exotic spices, dried fruits, and preserved fruits were brought to Europe by the expansion of trade routes. Fruitcake recipes were developed as a result, becoming more complex and tasty. Fruitcakes became a symbol of joy and were frequently consumed at weddings and other special events.

Christian Traditions: Fruitcakes are closely associated with Christianity, especially during Christmas. Fruitcakes were seen to be a good choice for religious feasts and rites because of their dense and durable nature. With its mixture of fruits, spices, and alcohol, the Christmas fruitcake evolved into a global holiday favorite.

Colonial America: Fruitcake customs were introduced to the Americas by European settlers. American-style fruitcakes were created by modifying fruitcake recipes to fit local tastes and ingredient availability. These cakes frequently had a variety of fruits and nuts along with a lighter texture.

Victorian age: In England, the Victorian age improved the technique of making fruitcakes. Wedding fruitcakes with elaborate decorations, frequently adorned with marzipan and elaborate patterns, came to represent luxury and festivity.

International Variations: Different cultures have different perspectives on fruitcakes. For instance, the German Stollen is a buttery, fruit-filled bread, and the Italian Panforte is a spicy, chewy variation. The Caribbean is home to fruitcakes that are rich and dark, such as Black Cake, which is a popular option for celebratory events.

World Wars and Rationing: Due to rationing and ingredient shortages, fruitcake recipes changed during the World Wars. Due to the need to modify their recipes to fit their limited resources, home bakers created variants such as the "war cake."

Modern Adaptations: Fruitcakes have changed over the years to accommodate different nutritional requirements. Fruitcakes that are nut-free, gluten-free, and vegan are becoming more and more popular, so a larger audience can savor these delicious delicacies.

Continued Tradition: Fruitcakes are still loved and eaten worldwide, despite being the target of ridicule and misunderstandings. Whether they are served as wedding cakes, Christmas fruitcakes, or other special occasion treats, they continue to play an important role in celebrations.

Fruitcakes' long history bears witness to their enduring appeal; throughout the ages, they have changed and adjusted to accommodate shifting societal norms and tastes. Fruitcakes, no matter how sophisticated or basic, traditional or contemporary, continue to represent happiness, festivities, and the transferring of culinary customs between the generations.

Essential Ingredients For Making Non Alcoholic Fruitcake

1. **Mixed Dried Fruits**: A blend of dried fruits, including dates, figs, raisins, currants, and apricots, adds a range of flavors and textures in addition to natural sweetness.

2. **Chopped Nuts**: Almonds, walnuts, and pecans give the fruitcake a delicious crunch and nutty flavor.

3. **All-Purpose Flour**: This gives the cake batter structure and a crumbly, light texture. It is used as the foundation for the batter.

4. **Baking Powder**: A leavening agent, baking powder aids in the cake's rising and fluff.

5. **Baking Soda**: Baking soda adds texture to the cake and helps with leavening.

6. **Spices**: To infuse the cake with warm, fragrant flavors, ground spices such as cloves, cinnamon, nutmeg, and allspice are important.

7. **Butter**: The cake gets more moisture and richness with unsalted butter.

8. **Brown Sugar**: Brown sugar gives the fruitcake sweetness and a rich flavor.

9. **Eggs**: These provide structure and act as a binding agent, keeping the cake together.

10. **Unsweetened Applesauce**: Applesauce gives the fruitcake natural sweetness, flavor, and moisture. It also serves as a non-alcoholic substitute for alcohol.

11. **Vanilla Extract**: The flavor profile of the cake is improved overall by the use of vanilla extract.

12. **Citrus Zest**: To provide a zesty burst of freshness, zest from lemon and orange can be added.

For those who would rather not use alcohol in their recipes, these ingredients combine to make a delectable non-alcoholic fruitcake. Additionally, you can customize the fruitcake to your preferences by experimenting with different nuts and dried fruits.

Essential Tools For Making Non Alcoholic Fruitcake

1. **Mixing Bowls**: A variety of bowl sizes for blending and prepping items.

2. **Electric Mixer or Hand Held Whisk**: Use this tool to fully combine the batter, beat the eggs, and cream the butter and sugar.

3. **Spatula**: To fold in ingredients and scrape down the sides of the basin.

Measuring Cups and Spoons: To measure wet and dry components precisely.

5. **Baking Pans** : Bake the fruitcake in a cake tin or loaf pan.

6. **Parchment Paper**: To make taking out the cake simpler, line the baking pan.

7. **Cooling Rack**: After baking, the fruitcake is cooled on a wire rack.

8. **Oven**: Let the fruitcake bake and preheat.

9. **Fine-mesh sieve or sifter**: Used to filter out dry components like spices and flour.

10. **Zester or Microplane**: For a taste boost, zest citrus fruits.

11. **Knife and Cutting Board**: Used to chop the almonds and dried fruits.

12. Use a wooden spoon or whisk instead of an electric mixer to combine ingredients.

13. **Plastic or Aluminum Foil**: To store and package the fruitcake.

To prepare, bake, and cool your non-alcoholic fruitcake, you'll need these tools. The efficiency and enjoyment of baking can be increased by having the appropriate tools available.

Tips For Making Non Alcoholic Fruitcakes

Attention to detail and tried-and-true processes are required for the ultimate non-alcoholic fruitcake. Here are some pointers to help you get a tasty result:

1. **High-Quality components**: To create a tasty and fulfilling fruitcake, begin with the highest quality dried fruits, nuts, and other components.

2. **Ingredients at Room Temperature**: Make sure your butter and eggs are at room temperature.

This allows them to blend more easily, resulting in a more uniform batter.

3. **Proper Mixing**: Thoroughly cream the butter and sugar until the mixture is light and fluffy. This process contributes to a soft cake texture.

4. **Even Ingredient Distribution**: When adding the dried fruits and nuts, ensure sure they are dispersed equally throughout the batter. This guarantees that each slice of fruitcake has a well-balanced taste profile.

5. **Sift Dry Ingredients**: Sifting dry ingredients such as flour and spices helps to avoid lumps and ensures that the spices are evenly distributed in the batter.

6. **Preheat the Oven**: Always preheat the oven to the temperature stated before inserting the fruitcake. Even baking is ensured by a properly prepared oven.

7. **Use the Correct Pan**: Use the pan size and type stated in your recipe. A good baking pan ensures consistent baking and prevents overcooking or undercooking.

8. **Parchment Paper Lining**: Line the baking pan with parchment paper to make it simpler to remove the fruitcake once it's finished baking.

9. **Slow Baking**: Fruitcakes are notorious for taking a long time to bake. This allows the tastes to develop and mingle. For the best results, bake at the prescribed temperature and time.

10. **Check for Doneness**: Insert a toothpick or cake tester into the middle of the fruitcake to see whether it is done. The cake is done when it comes out clean or with only a few wet crumbs. Keep an eye on the baking time because it will vary depending on your oven and pan size.

11. **Cool Gradually**: Allow the fruitcake to cool in the pan for about 10-15 minutes after removing it from the oven. After that, place it on a wire rack to cool entirely. This progressive cooling aids in the preservation of the cake's texture.

12. **Aging (Optional)**: To enable the flavors to merge and develop over time, cover the cooled fruitcake in plastic wrap or aluminum foil and keep it in a cold, dry area. Some folks also like to "feed" the cake with apple juice or non-alcoholic syrup.

13. **How to Store**: To keep your non-alcoholic fruit cake fresh, store it in an airtight container. Depending on your preferences, it may be stored at room temperature or in the refrigerator.

You can make a moist, delicious, and rich non-alcoholic fruitcake by following these instructions. Experiment with various fruit and nut combinations to make your own distinctive fruitcake that meets your tastes.

Chapter 2:

Non Alcoholic Fruitcakes

Non Alcoholic English Christmas fruitcakes

1. Christmas Spice Delight Fruitcake

Ingredients:
- 1 cup dried fruit mixture (raisins, currants, sultanas)
- 1/2 cup candied peel, chopped
- 1/2 cup glace cherries, chopped
- 1/2 cup dried apricots, chopped
- 1/2 cup chopped nuts (almonds or walnuts)
- 1 1/2 cups regular flour
- 1 pound unsalted butter
- 1 pound brown sugar
- 2 medium eggs
- 1/2 cup plain applesauce
1 teaspoon ground cinnamon

1/2 teaspoon ground nutmeg

1/2 teaspoon baking powder

Preparation:

1. Preheat the oven to 325 degrees Fahrenheit (165 degrees Celsius). Line an 8-inch round cake pan with parchment paper and grease it.

2. Cream the butter and brown sugar together in a large mixing basin until light and creamy. Beat in the eggs one at a time, beating well after each addition.

3. Combine the flour, cinnamon, nutmeg, and baking powder in a separate basin. Add the dry ingredients to the wet mixture gradually, mixing until just mixed.

4. Combine the dried fruits, candied peel, cherries, apricots, and almonds in a mixing bowl.

5. Smooth the top of the batter into the prepared cake pan.

6. Bake for 1.5–2 hours, or until a toothpick inserted in the middle comes out clean. Allow the cake to cool for 15 minutes in the pan before transferring to a wire rack to cool entirely.

2. Traditional Yuletide Bliss Fruitcake

Ingredients:

- 2 cup dried fruit mixture (raisins, currants, sultanas)
- 1/2 cup candied peel, chopped
- 1/2 cup dried apricots, chopped
- 1/2 cup chopped nuts (almonds or pecans)
- 2 1/2 cups regular flour

1 pound unsalted butter

granulated sugar 1 cup

- four big eggs
- 1/2 cup plain applesauce

1 teaspoon ground cinnamon

1/2 teaspoon ground allspice

1/2 teaspoon baking soda

Preparation:

1. Preheat the oven to 300 degrees Fahrenheit (150 degrees Celsius). Line a 9-inch round cake pan with parchment paper and grease it.

2. Cream the butter and sugar together in a large mixing basin until light and creamy. Beat in the eggs one at a time, beating well after each addition.

3. Combine the flour, cinnamon, allspice, and baking soda in a separate basin. Add the dry ingredients to the wet mixture gradually, mixing until just mixed.

4. Fold in the dried fruit mixture, candied peel, apricots, and nuts.

5. Smooth the top of the batter into the prepared cake pan.

6. Cook for 2.5–3 hours, or until a toothpick inserted into the middle comes out clean. Allow the cake to cool for 30 minutes in the pan before transferring to a wire rack to cool entirely.

3. Cake with Apple Harvest Jewels

Ingredients:

- 1 1/2 cup dried fruit mixture (raisins, currants, sultanas)
- 1/2 cup candied peel, chopped
- 1/2 cup glace cherries, chopped
- 1/2 cup dried figs, chopped
- 1/2 cup pecans, chopped
- 2 cups regular flour
- 1 pound unsalted butter
- 1 pound brown sugar
- three big eggs
- 1/2 cup plain applesauce
1 teaspoon ground ginger
1/2 teaspoon ground cloves
1/2 teaspoon baking powder

Preparation:

1. Preheat the oven to 325 degrees Fahrenheit (165 degrees Celsius). Line a 9-inch square cake pan with parchment paper and grease it.

2. Cream the butter and brown sugar together in a large mixing basin until light and creamy. Beat in the eggs one at a time, beating well after each addition.

3. Combine the flour, ginger, cloves, and baking powder in a separate basin. Add the dry ingredients to the wet mixture gradually, mixing until just mixed.

4. Combine the dried fruits, candied peel, cherries, figs, and pecans in a mixing bowl.

5. Smooth the top of the batter into the prepared cake pan.

6. Bake for 1.5–2 hours, or until a toothpick inserted in the middle comes out clean. Allow the cake to cool for 15 minutes in the pan before transferring to a wire rack to cool entirely.

4. Winter Wonder Cake with Walnuts

Ingredients:
- 1 1/2 cup dried fruit mixture (raisins, currants, sultanas)
- 1/2 cup candied peel, chopped
- 1/2 cup dried apricots, chopped
- 1/2 cup walnuts, chopped
- 1 1/2 cups regular flour
- 1 pound unsalted butter
granulated sugar, 1/2 cup
- three big eggs
- 1/2 cup plain applesauce
1 teaspoon ground cinnamon
1/2 teaspoon ground nutmeg
1/2 teaspoon baking powder

Preparation:
1. Preheat the oven to 325 degrees Fahrenheit (165 degrees Celsius). Line an 8-inch round cake pan with parchment paper and grease it.

2. Cream the butter and sugar together in a large mixing basin until light and creamy. Beat in the eggs one at a time, beating well after each addition.

3. Combine the flour, cinnamon, nutmeg, and baking powder in a separate basin. Add the dry ingredients to the wet mixture gradually, mixing until just mixed.

4. Fold in the dried fruit mixture, candied peel, apricots, and walnuts.

5. Smooth the top of the batter into the prepared cake pan.

6. Bake for 1.5–2 hours, or until a toothpick inserted in the middle comes out clean. Allow the cake to cool for 15 minutes in the pan before transferring to a wire rack to cool entirely.

5. Christmas Loaf Citrus Sensation

Ingredients:

- 1 1/2 cup dried fruit mixture (raisins, currants, sultanas)
- 1/2 cup candied peel, chopped
- 1/2 cup dried apricots, chopped
- 1/2 cup almonds, chopped

- 2 cups regular flour
- 1 pound unsalted butter
- 1 pound brown sugar
- three big eggs
- 1/2 cup plain applesauce
1 teaspoon grated orange zest
- 1/2 teaspoon lemon zest
1/2 teaspoon baking powder

Preparation:

1. Preheat the oven to 325 degrees Fahrenheit (165 degrees Celsius). Line an 8-inch loaf pan with parchment paper and grease it.

2. Cream the butter and brown sugar together in a large mixing basin until light and creamy. Beat in the eggs one at a time, beating well after each addition.

3. In a second dish, whisk together the flour, orange zest, lemon zest, and baking powder. Add the dry ingredients to the wet mixture gradually, mixing until just mixed.

4. Fold in the dried fruit mixture, candied peel, apricots, and almonds.

5. Smooth the top of the batter into the prepared loaf pan.

6. Bake for 1.5–2 hours, or until a toothpick inserted in the middle comes out clean. Allow the loaf to cool for 15 minutes in the pan before transferring to a wire rack to cool entirely.

6. Cake with Nutty Pineapple Paradise

Ingredients:
- 2 cup dried fruit mixture (raisins, currants, sultanas)
- 1/2 cup candied peel, chopped
- 1/2 cup glace cherries, chopped
- 1/2 cup dried apricots, chopped
- 1/2 cup pineapple chunks, chopped
- 2 1/2 cups regular flour
1 pound unsalted butter
granulated sugar 1 cup

- four big eggs
- 1/2 cup plain applesauce

1 teaspoon ground cinnamon

1/2 teaspoon ground nutmeg

1/2 teaspoon baking soda

Preparation:

1. Preheat the oven to 300 degrees Fahrenheit (150 degrees Celsius). Line a 9-inch round cake pan with parchment paper and grease it.

2. Cream the butter and sugar together in a large mixing basin until light and creamy. Beat in the eggs one at a time, beating well after each addition.

3. Combine the flour, cinnamon, nutmeg, and baking soda in a separate basin. Add the dry ingredients to the wet mixture gradually, mixing until just mixed.

4. Combine the dried fruits, candied peel, cherries, apricots, pineapple chunks, and almonds in a mixing bowl.

5. Smooth the top of the batter into the prepared cake pan.

6. Cook for 2.5–3 hours, or until a toothpick inserted into the middle comes out clean. Allow the cake to cool for 30 minutes in the pan before transferring to a wire rack to cool entirely.

© Love and Confections

7. Comfortable Coffee Pecan Loaf

Ingredients:

- 1 1/2 cup dried fruit mixture (raisins, currants, sultanas)
- 1/2 cup candied peel, chopped
- 1/2 cup dried apricots, chopped
- 1/2 cup pecans, chopped
- 1 1/2 cups regular flour
- 1 pound unsalted butter
- 1 pound brown sugar
- three big eggs
- 1/2 cup plain applesauce
1 teaspoon ground cinnamon
1/2 teaspoon ground coffee
1/2 teaspoon baking powder

Preparation:

1. Preheat the oven to 325 degrees Fahrenheit (165 degrees Celsius). Line an 8-inch loaf pan with parchment paper and grease it.

2. Cream the butter and brown sugar together in a large mixing basin until light and creamy. Beat in the eggs one at a time, beating well after each addition.

3. Combine the flour, ground coffee, and baking powder in a separate basin. Add the dry ingredients to the wet mixture gradually, mixing until just mixed.

4. Fold in the dried fruit mixture, candied peel, apricots, and pecans.

5. Smooth the top of the batter into the prepared loaf pan.

6. Bake for 1.5–2 hours, or until a toothpick inserted in the middle comes out clean. Allow the loaf to cool for 15 minutes in the pan before transferring to a wire rack to cool entirely.

Non Alcoholic American-style fruitcake

1. Southern Pecan Fruitcake

Ingredients:

- 2 cup dry fruit mix (raisins, currants, dates)
- 1 cup pecans, chopped
- 2 1/2 cups regular flour

1 pound unsalted butter

granulated sugar 1 cup

- four big eggs
- 1/2 cup plain applesauce

1 teaspoon ground cinnamon

1/2 teaspoon ground allspice

1/2 teaspoon baking soda

Preparation:

1. Preheat the oven to 325 degrees Fahrenheit (165 degrees Celsius). Line a 9-inch round cake pan with parchment paper and grease it.

2. Cream the butter and sugar together in a large mixing basin until light and creamy. Beat in the eggs one at a time, beating well after each addition.

3. Combine the flour, cinnamon, allspice, and baking soda in a separate basin. Add the dry ingredients to the wet mixture gradually, mixing until just mixed.

4. Mix in the dried fruits and pecans.

5. Smooth the top of the batter into the prepared cake pan.

6. Cook for 2.5–3 hours, or until a toothpick inserted into the middle comes out clean. Allow the cake to cool for 30 minutes in the pan before transferring to a wire rack to cool entirely.

2.Fruitcake with Nutty Banana Bliss

Ingredients:
- 2 cup dry fruit mix (raisins, currants, dates)
- 1 cup walnuts, chopped
- 2 1/2 cups regular flour
1 pound unsalted butter
granulated sugar 1 cup
- 4 mashed ripe bananas
- three big eggs
1 teaspoon ground cinnamon
1/2 teaspoon ground nutmeg
1/2 teaspoon baking powder

Preparation:
1. Preheat the oven to 325 degrees Fahrenheit (165 degrees Celsius). Line a 9-inch round cake pan with parchment paper and grease it.
2. Cream the butter and sugar together in a large mixing basin until light and creamy. Beat in the eggs one at a time, beating well after each addition.
3. Incorporate the mashed bananas.

4. Combine the flour, cinnamon, nutmeg, and baking powder in a separate basin. Add the dry ingredients to the wet mixture gradually, mixing until just mixed.

5. Fold in the chopped walnuts and dried fruits.

6. Smooth the top of the batter into the prepared cake pan.

7. Cook for 2.5–3 hours, or until a toothpick inserted into the middle comes out clean. Allow the cake to cool for 30 minutes in the pan before transferring to a wire rack to cool entirely.

3. Festive Citrus Celebration Cake

Ingredients:

- 2 cup dry fruit mix (raisins, currants, dates)
- 1/2 cup candied orange peel, chopped
- 1/2 cup candied lemon peel, chopped
- 1 cup pecans, chopped
- 2 1/2 cups regular flour

1 pound unsalted butter

granulated sugar 1 cup

- four big eggs
- 1/2 cup plain applesauce

1 teaspoon grated orange zest

- 1/2 teaspoon lemon zest

1/2 teaspoon baking soda

Preparation:

1. Preheat the oven to 300 degrees Fahrenheit (150 degrees Celsius). Line a 9-inch round cake pan with parchment paper and grease it.

2. Cream the butter and sugar together in a large mixing basin until light and creamy. Beat in the eggs one at a time, beating well after each addition.

3. Incorporate the orange and lemon zests.

4. Combine the flour and baking soda in a separate basin. Add the dry ingredients to the wet mixture gradually, mixing until just mixed.

5. Combine the dried fruits, candied orange peel, candied lemon peel, and pecans in a mixing bowl.

6. Smooth the top of the batter into the prepared cake pan.

7. Cook for 2.5–3 hours, or until a toothpick inserted into the middle comes out clean. Allow the cake to cool for 30 minutes in the pan before transferring to a wire rack to cool entirely.

4. Tropical Pineapple Paradise

Ingredients:

- 2 cup dry fruit mix (raisins, currants, dates)
- 1/2 cup candied pineapple, chopped
- 1/2 cup coconut shredded
- 1 cup walnuts, chopped
- 2 1/2 cups regular flour

1 pound unsalted butter

granulated sugar 1 cup

- four big eggs
- 1/2 cup plain applesauce

1 teaspoon grated orange zest

- 1/2 teaspoon lemon zest

1/2 teaspoon baking powder

Preparation:

1. Preheat the oven to 325 degrees Fahrenheit (165 degrees Celsius). Line a 9-inch round cake pan with parchment paper and grease it.

2. Cream the butter and sugar together in a large mixing basin until light and creamy. Beat in the eggs one at a time, beating well after each addition.

3. Incorporate the orange and lemon zests.

4. Combine the flour and baking powder in a separate basin. Add the dry ingredients to the wet mixture gradually, mixing until just mixed.

5. Mix in the dried fruits, candied pineapple, shredded coconut, and walnuts.

6. Smooth the top of the batter into the prepared cake pan.

7. Cook for 2.5–3 hours, or until a toothpick inserted into the middle comes out clean. Allow the cake to cool for 30 minutes in the pan before transferring to a wire rack to cool entirely.

5. Cranberry Cinnamon Swirl

Ingredients:

- 1 1/2 cup dry fruit mixture (raisins, currants, dates)
- 1 cup cranberries, dried
- 1/2 cup walnuts, chopped
- 2 cups regular flour
- 1 pound unsalted butter
- 1 pound brown sugar
- three big eggs
- 1/2 cup plain applesauce

1 teaspoon ground cinnamon

1/2 teaspoon ground nutmeg

1/2 teaspoon baking powder

Preparation:

1. Preheat the oven to 325 degrees Fahrenheit (165 degrees Celsius). Line a 9-inch round cake pan with parchment paper and grease it.

2. Cream the butter and brown sugar together in a large mixing basin until light and creamy. Beat in the eggs one at a time, beating well after each addition.

3. Combine the flour, cinnamon, nutmeg, and baking powder in a separate basin. Add the dry ingredients to the wet mixture gradually, mixing until just mixed.

4. Fold in the dried mixed fruits, cranberries, and walnuts.

5. Half of the batter should be poured into the prepared cake pan.

6. Combine 1 tablespoon ground cinnamon and 2 tablespoons granulated sugar in a small mixing basin. Half of the cinnamon-sugar mixture should be sprinkled over the batter in the pan.

7. Sprinkle the leftover cinnamon-sugar mixture on top of the remaining batter.

8. Cook for 2.5–3 hours, or until a toothpick inserted into the middle comes out clean. Allow the cake to cool for 30 minutes in the pan before transferring to a wire rack to cool entirely.

6.Chocolate Cherry Delight

Ingredients:

- 1 1/2 cup dry fruit mixture (raisins, currants, dates)
- half a cup dried cherries
- 1/2 cup pecans, chopped
- 2 cups regular flour
- 1 pound unsalted butter

granulated sugar, 1/2 cup

- three big eggs
- 1/2 cup plain applesauce
- half a cup cocoa powder

1/2 teaspoon baking powder

Preparation:

1. Preheat the oven to 325 degrees Fahrenheit (165 degrees Celsius). Line a 9-inch round cake pan with parchment paper and grease it.

2. Cream the butter and sugar together in a large mixing basin until light and creamy. Beat in the eggs one at a time, beating well after each addition.

3. Incorporate the cocoa powder.

4. Combine the flour and baking powder in a separate basin. Add the dry ingredients to the wet mixture gradually, mixing until just mixed.

5. Fold in the dried fruit mixture, dried cherries, and chopped pecans.

6. Smooth the top of the batter into the prepared cake pan.

7. Cook for 2.5–3 hours, or until a toothpick inserted into the middle comes out clean. Allow the cake to cool for 30 minutes in the pan before transferring to a wire rack to cool entirely.

7. Cinnamon Apple Pecan Cake

Ingredients:

- 1 1/2 cup dry fruit mixture (raisins, currants, dates)
- 1 cup dried apple chunks
- 1/2 cup pecans, chopped
- 2 cups regular flour
- 1 pound unsalted butter
- 1 pound brown sugar
- three big eggs
- 1/2 cup plain applesauce

1 teaspoon ground cinnamon

1/2 teaspoon ground nutmeg

1/2 teaspoon baking powder

Preparation:

1. Preheat the oven to 325 degrees Fahrenheit (165 degrees Celsius). Line a 9-inch round cake pan with parchment paper and grease it.

2. Cream the butter and brown sugar together in a large mixing basin until light and creamy. Beat in the eggs one at a time, beating well after each addition.

3. Combine the flour, cinnamon, nutmeg, and baking powder in a separate basin. Add the dry ingredients to the wet mixture gradually, mixing until just mixed.

4. Mix in the dried fruits, apple chunks, and chopped pecans.

5. Smooth the top of the batter into the prepared cake pan.

6. Cook for 2.5–3 hours, or until a toothpick inserted into the middle comes out clean. Allow the cake to cool for 30 minutes in the pan before transferring to a wire rack to cool entirely.

8. Nutty Walnut Harvest Cake

Ingredients:
- 2 cup dry fruit mix (raisins, currants, dates)
- 1/2 cup candied peel, chopped
- 1 cup walnuts, chopped
- 2 1/2 cups regular flour
1 pound unsalted butter
granulated sugar 1 cup
- four big eggs
- 1/2 cup plain applesauce
1 teaspoon ground cinnamon
1/2 teaspoon ground allspice
1/2 teaspoon baking soda

Preparation:

1. Preheat the oven to 300 degrees Fahrenheit (150 degrees Celsius). Line a 9-inch round cake pan with parchment paper and grease it.

2. Cream the butter and sugar together in a large mixing basin until light and creamy. Beat in the eggs one at a time, beating well after each addition.

3. Combine the flour, cinnamon, allspice, and baking soda in a separate basin. Add the dry ingredients to the wet mixture gradually, mixing until just mixed.

4. Fold in the dry fruit mixture, candied peel, and walnuts.

5. Smooth the top of the batter into the prepared cake pan.

6. Cook for 2.5–3 hours, or until a toothpick inserted into the middle comes out clean. Allow the cake to cool for 30 minutes in the pan before transferring to a wire rack to cool entirely.

Non-alcoholic Southern Pecan Fruitcakes

1. Southern Pecan Harvest Delight Cake

Ingredients:

- 2 cup pecan halves
- 1 1/2 cup dried fruits (raisins, currants, sultanas)
- 1/2 cup candied pecans
- 1 1/2 cups regular flour
1 pound unsalted butter
1 cup of brown sugar
- four big eggs
1 teaspoon ground cinnamon
- 1/2 cup unsweetened applesauce
1/2 teaspoon ground nutmeg
1/2 teaspoon baking powder

Preparation:

1. Preheat the oven to 325 degrees Fahrenheit (165 degrees Celsius). Line a 9-inch round cake pan with parchment paper and grease it.

2. Cream the butter and brown sugar together in a large mixing basin until light and fluffy. Beat in the eggs one at a time, beating well after each addition.

3. Combine the flour, cinnamon, nutmeg, and baking powder in a separate basin. Add the dry ingredients to the wet mixture gradually, mixing until just mixed.

4. Combine the pecan halves, mixed dry fruits, candied pecans, and applesauce in a mixing bowl.

5. Smooth the top of the batter into the prepared cake pan.

6. Bake for 2.5 to 3 hours, or until a toothpick inserted into the center of the cake comes out clean. Allow the cake to cool for 30 minutes in the pan before transferring to a wire rack to cool entirely.

2. Georgia Pecan Oasis Cake

Ingredients:

- 2 cup pecan halves
  - 1 1/2 cup dried fruits (raisins, currants, sultanas)
  - 1/2 cup candied pecans
- 1 1/2 cups regular flour
1 pound unsalted butter
1 cup of granulated sugar 4 big eggs
1 teaspoon ground cinnamon
- 1/2 cup unsweetened applesauce
1/2 teaspoon ground allspice
1/2 teaspoon baking soda

Preparation:

1. Preheat the oven to 300 degrees Fahrenheit (150 degrees Celsius). Line a 9-inch round cake pan with parchment paper and grease it.

2. Cream the butter and sugar together in a large mixing basin until light and fluffy. Beat in the eggs one at a time, beating well after each addition.

3. Combine the flour, cinnamon, allspice, and baking soda in a separate basin. Add the dry ingredients to the wet mixture gradually, mixing until just mixed.

4. Combine the pecan halves, mixed dry fruits, candied pecans, and applesauce in a mixing bowl.

5. Smooth the top of the batter into the prepared cake pan.

6. Bake for 3 to 3.5 hours, or until a toothpick inserted into the center of the cake comes out clean. Allow the cake to cool for 30 minutes in the pan before transferring to a wire rack to cool entirely.

3. Magnolia Pecan Spice Cake

Ingredients:

1 1/2 cups pecan halves 1 cup dried fruits (raisins, currants, sultanas) 1/2 cup candied pecans

- 1 1/2 cups regular flour

- 1 pound unsalted butter

- 1 pound brown sugar

- three big eggs

- 1/2 cup plain applesauce

1 teaspoon ground ginger, 1/2 teaspoon ground cloves

1/2 teaspoon baking powder

Preparation:

1. Preheat the oven to 325 degrees Fahrenheit (165 degrees Celsius). Line a 9-inch round cake pan with parchment paper and grease it.

2. Cream the butter and brown sugar together in a large mixing basin until light and fluffy. Beat in the eggs one at a time, beating well after each addition.

3. Combine the flour, ginger, cloves, and baking powder in a separate basin. Add the dry ingredients to the wet mixture gradually, mixing until just mixed.

4. Combine the pecan halves, mixed dry fruits, candied pecans, and applesauce in a mixing bowl.

5. Smooth the top of the batter into the prepared cake pan.

6. Bake for 2 to 2.5 hours, or until a toothpick inserted into the center of the cake comes out clean. Allow the cake to cool for 30 minutes in the pan before transferring to a wire rack to cool entirely.

4. Pecan Cake with Southern Comfort

Ingredients:

- 2 cups halved pecans
- 1 cup dried fruit mixture (raisins, currants, sultanas)
- 1/2 cup candied pecans, chopped
- 1 1/2 cup unsalted butter
- 1/2 cup granulated sugar
- 4 big eggs
1 teaspoon ground cinnamon
- 1/2 cup unsweetened applesauce
- 1/2 teaspoon powdered nutmeg
- 1/2 teaspoon baking soda

Preparation:

1. Preheat the oven to 300 degrees Fahrenheit (150 degrees Celsius). Line a 9-inch round cake pan with parchment paper and grease it.

2. Cream the butter and sugar together in a large mixing basin until light and fluffy. Beat in the eggs one at a time, beating well after each addition.

3. Combine the flour, cinnamon, nutmeg, and baking soda in a separate basin. Add the dry ingredients to the wet mixture gradually, mixing until just mixed.

4. Combine the pecan halves, mixed dry fruits, candied pecans, and applesauce in a mixing bowl.

5. Smooth the top of the batter into the prepared cake pan.

6. Bake for 3 to 3.5 hours, or until a toothpick inserted into the center of the cake comes out clean. Allow the cake to cool for 30 minutes in the pan before transferring to a wire rack to cool entirely.

5. Pecan Orchard Spice Loaf

Ingredients:
-1 1/2 cups pecan halves 1 cup dried fruits (raisins, currants, sultanas)
- 1/2 cup candied pecans
- 1 1/2 cups regular flour
- 1 pound unsalted butter
- 1 pound brown sugar
- three big eggs
- 1/2 cup plain applesauce
-1 teaspoon powdered cinnamon
- 1/2 teaspoon ground nutmeg
-1/2 teaspoon baking powder

Preparation:
1. Preheat the oven to 325 degrees Fahrenheit (165 degrees Celsius). Line a 9-inch round cake pan with parchment paper and grease it.
2. Cream the butter and brown sugar together in a large mixing basin until light and fluffy. Beat in the eggs one at a time, beating well after each addition.

3. Combine the flour, cinnamon, nutmeg, and baking powder in a separate basin. Add the dry ingredients to the wet mixture gradually, mixing until just mixed.

4. Combine the pecan halves, mixed dry fruits, candied pecans, and applesauce in a mixing bowl.

5. Smooth the top of the batter into the prepared cake pan.

6. Bake for 2 to 2.5 hours, or until a toothpick inserted into the center of the cake comes out clean. Allow the cake to cool for 30 minutes in the pan before transferring to a wire rack to cool entirely.

Non Alcoholic Caribbean Black Cake

1. Tropical Paradise Black Cake

Ingredients:
- 1 cup chopped candied pineapple
- 1 cup candied cherries
- 2 cups assorted dried fruits (raisins, currants, prunes)
- 1 1/2 cups regular flour
1 pound unsalted butter
1 cup of brown sugar
- four big eggs
- 1/4 cup molasses
- 1/2 cup unsweetened applesauce
1 teaspoon ground allspice
1/2 teaspoon ground nutmeg
1/2 teaspoon baking powder

Preparation:

1. Preheat the oven to 300 degrees Fahrenheit (150 degrees Celsius). Line a 9-inch round cake pan with parchment paper and grease it.

2. Cream the butter and brown sugar together in a large mixing basin until light and fluffy. Beat in the eggs one at a time, beating well after each addition.

3. Combine the flour, allspice, nutmeg, and baking powder in a separate basin. Add the dry ingredients to the wet mixture gradually, mixing until just mixed.

4. Stir in the dry fruit mixture, candied pineapple, candied cherries, applesauce, and molasses.

5. Smooth the top of the batter into the prepared cake pan.

6. Bake for 3 to 3.5 hours, or until a toothpick inserted into the center of the cake comes out clean. Allow the cake to cool for 30 minutes in the pan before transferring to a wire rack to cool entirely.

2. Island Breeze Black Cake

Ingredients:

- 1 1/2 cups dried fruits mixed (raisins, currants, prunes)
- 1/2 cup candied ginger
- 1/2 cup candied papaya
- 1 1/2 cups regular flour
- 1 pound unsalted butter
½ cup of granulated sugar
- three big eggs
1 teaspoon ground cloves
- 1/2 cup unsweetened applesauce
- 1/4 cup honey
- 1/2 teaspoon cinnamon
- 1/2 teaspoon baking soda

Preparation:

1. Preheat the oven to 325 degrees Fahrenheit (165 degrees Celsius). Line a 9-inch round cake pan with parchment paper and grease it.

2. Cream the butter and sugar together in a large mixing basin until light and fluffy. Beat in the eggs one at a time, beating well after each addition.

3. Combine the flour, cloves, cinnamon, and baking soda in a separate basin. Add the dry ingredients to the wet mixture gradually, mixing until just mixed.

4. Stir in the dried fruit mixture, candied ginger, candied papaya, applesauce, and honey.

5. Smooth the top of the batter into the prepared cake pan.

6. Bake for 2.5 to 3 hours, or until a toothpick inserted into the center of the cake comes out clean. Allow the cake to cool for 30 minutes in the pan before transferring to a wire rack to cool entirely.

3. Black Cake with Caribbean Sunset

Ingredients:
- 1 cup chopped candied mango
- 1 cup candied orange peel
- 2 cups assorted dried fruits (raisins, currants, apricots)
- 1 1/2 cups regular flour

1 pound unsalted butter

1 cup of brown sugar
- four big eggs

1 teaspoon grated nutmeg

- 1/2 cup unsweetened applesauce

- 1/4 cup agave nectar

- 1/2 teaspoon of powdered ginger

- 1/2 teaspoon of baking powder

Preparation:

1. Preheat the oven to 300 degrees Fahrenheit (150 degrees Celsius). Line a 9-inch round cake pan with parchment paper and grease it.

2. Cream the butter and brown sugar together in a large mixing basin until light and fluffy. Beat in the eggs one at a time, beating well after each addition.

3. Combine the flour, nutmeg, ginger, and baking powder in a separate basin. Add the dry ingredients to the wet mixture gradually, mixing until just mixed.

4. Stir in the dry fruit mixture, candied mango, candied orange peel, applesauce, and agave nectar.

5. Smooth the top of the batter into the prepared cake pan.

6. Bake for 3 to 3.5 hours, or until a toothpick inserted into the center of the cake comes out clean. Allow the cake to cool for 30 minutes in the pan before transferring to a wire rack to cool entirely.

4. Black Cake Reggae Rhythms

Ingredients:

- 1 1/2 cups dried fruits mixed (raisins, currants, figs)
- 1/2 cup candied guava
- 1/2 cup candied passion fruit
- 1 1/2 cups regular flour
- 1 pound unsalted butter
-⅓ grcup ofgranulated sugar
- three big eggs
- 1/2 cup plain applesauce
- 1 tablespoon maple syrup
1 teaspoon ground allspice
1/2 teaspoon ground cinnamon
1/2 teaspoon baking soda

Preparation:

1. Preheat the oven to 325 degrees Fahrenheit (165 degrees Celsius). Line a 9-inch round cake pan with parchment paper and grease it.

2. Cream the butter and sugar together in a large mixing basin until light and fluffy. Beat in the eggs one at a time, beating well after each addition.

3. Combine the flour, allspice, cinnamon, and baking soda in a separate basin. Add the dry ingredients to the wet mixture gradually, mixing until just mixed.

4. Stir in the dried fruit mixture, candied guava, candied passion fruit, applesauce, and maple syrup.

5. Smooth the top of the batter into the prepared cake pan.

6. Bake for 2.5 to 3 hours, or until a toothpick inserted into the center of the cake comes out clean. Allow the cake to cool for 30 minutes in the pan before transferring to a wire rack to cool entirely.

5. Black Calypso Celebration Cake

Ingredients:
- 1 cup chopped candied coconut
- 2 cups assorted dried fruits (raisins, currants, dates)
1 cup of candied mango
- 1 1/2 cups regular flour
1 pound unsalted butter
1 cup of brown sugar
- four big eggs
- 1/2 cup plain applesauce
- 1 tablespoon pineapple juice
1 teaspoon ground cloves
- 1/2 teaspoon grated nutmeg
-1/2 teaspoon baking powder

Preparation:
1. Preheat the oven to 300 degrees Fahrenheit (150 degrees Celsius). Line a 9-inch round cake pan with parchment paper and grease it.
2. Cream the butter and brown sugar together in a large mixing basin until light and fluffy. Beat in the eggs one at a time, beating well after each addition.
3. In a separate dish, whisk together the flour as well as cloves, nutmeg, and baking powder. Add the dry

ingredients to the wet mixture gradually, mixing until just mixed.

4. Stir in the dried fruit mixture, candied coconut, candied mango, applesauce, and pineapple juice.

5. Smooth the top of the batter into the prepared cake pan.

6. Bake for 3 to 3.5 hours, or until a toothpick inserted into the center of the cake comes out clean. Allow the cake to cool for 30 minutes in the pan before transferring to a wire rack to cool entirely.

Non-Alcoholic Traditional Fruitcake recipes

1. Nutty Orchard Delight Fruitcake

Ingredients:*
- 2 cup dry fruit mix (raisins, currants, dates)
- 1 cup mixed nuts (walnuts, pecans, almonds) chopped
- 1 1/2 cups regular flour
- 1 pound unsalted butter
- 1 pound brown sugar
- three big eggs
- 1/2 cup plain applesauce
1 teaspoon ground cinnamon
1/2 teaspoon ground allspice
1/2 teaspoon baking powder

Preparation:

1. Preheat the oven to 325 degrees Fahrenheit (165 degrees Celsius). Line a 9-inch round cake pan with parchment paper and grease it.

2. Cream the butter and brown sugar together in a large mixing basin until light and fluffy. Beat in the eggs one at a time, beating well after each addition.

3. Combine the flour, cinnamon, allspice, and baking powder in a separate basin. Add the dry ingredients to the wet mixture gradually, mixing until just mixed.

4. Stir in the dried fruits, nuts, and applesauce.

5. Smooth the top of the batter into the prepared cake pan.

6. Bake for 2.5 to 3 hours, or until a toothpick inserted into the center of the cake comes out clean. Allow the cake to cool for 30 minutes in the pan before transferring to a wire rack to cool entirely.

2. Traditional Holiday Nutcracker Fruitcake

Ingredients:

- 1 1/2 cup dried fruit mixture (raisins, currants, apricots)
- 1 cup mixed nuts, chopped (cashews, hazelnuts, pistachios)
- 1 1/2 cups regular flour
- 1 pound unsalted butter
-3 big eggs
- 1/2 cup granulated sugar
1 teaspoon ground nutmeg
- 1/2 cup unsweetened applesauce
- 1/4 cup honey
1/2 teaspoon ground cloves
1/2 teaspoon baking soda

Preparation:

1. Preheat the oven to 325 degrees Fahrenheit (165 degrees Celsius). Line a 9-inch round cake pan with parchment paper and grease it.

2. Cream the butter and sugar together in a large mixing basin until light and fluffy. Beat in the eggs one at a time, beating well after each addition.

3. Combine the flour, nutmeg, cloves, and baking soda in a separate basin. Add the dry ingredients to the wet mixture gradually, mixing until just mixed.

4. Stir in the dried fruits, almonds, applesauce, and honey.

5. Smooth the top of the batter into the prepared cake pan.

6. Bake for 2.5 to 3 hours, or until a toothpick inserted into the center of the cake comes out clean. Allow the cake to cool for 30 minutes in the pan before transferring to a wire rack to cool entirely.

3. Fruit and Nut Cake

Ingredients:
- 2 cup dried fruit mix (raisins, currants, figs)
- 1 cup chopped mixed nuts (macadamia nuts, Brazil nuts, and pine nuts)
- 1 1/2 cups regular flour
- 1 pound unsalted butter
- 1 pound brown sugar

- three big eggs
- 1/2 cup plain applesauce
1 teaspoon ground cinnamon
- 1/4 cup agave nectar
- 1/2 teaspoon of powdered ginger
- 1/2 teaspoon of baking powder

Preparation:

1. Preheat the oven to 325 degrees Fahrenheit (165 degrees Celsius). Line a 9-inch round cake pan with parchment paper and grease it.

2. Cream the butter and brown sugar together in a large mixing basin until light and fluffy. Beat in the eggs one at a time, beating well after each addition.

3. Combine the flour, cinnamon, ginger, and baking powder in a separate basin. Add the dry ingredients to the wet mixture gradually, mixing until just mixed.

4. Stir in the dried fruits, almonds, applesauce, and agave nectar.

5. Smooth the top of the batter into the prepared cake pan.

6. Bake for 2.5 to 3 hours, or until a toothpick inserted into the center of the cake comes out clean. Allow the cake to cool for 30 minutes in the pan before transferring to a wire rack to cool entirely.

4. Orchard Nut and Fruit Loaf for the Holidays

Ingredients:
- 1 1/2 cup dry fruit mixture (raisins, currants, dates)
- 1/2 cup mixed nuts (pecans, almonds, cashews) chopped
- 1 1/2 cups regular flour
- 1 pound unsalted butter
½ cup of granulated sugar
- three big eggs
- 1/2 cup plain applesauce
- 1 tablespoon maple syrup
1 teaspoon ground allspice
1/2 teaspoon ground cloves
1/2 teaspoon baking soda

Preparation:
1. Preheat the oven to 325 degrees Fahrenheit (165 degrees Celsius). Line a 9-inch round cake pan with parchment paper and grease it.
2. Cream the butter and sugar together in a large mixing basin until light and fluffy. Beat in the eggs one at a time, beating well after each addition.

3. Combine the flour, spices, cloves, and baking soda in a separate basin. Add the dry ingredients to the wet mixture gradually, mixing until just mixed.

4. Stir in the dried fruits, almonds, applesauce, and maple syrup.

5. Smooth the top of the batter into the prepared cake pan.

6. Bake for 2.5 to 3 hours, or until a toothpick inserted into the center of the cake comes out clean. Allow the cake to cool for 30 minutes in the pan before transferring to a wire rack to cool entirely.

5. Healthy Nut and Fruit Medley Cake

Ingredients:
- 1 cup chopped mixed nuts (walnuts, almonds, pistachios)
- 2 cups mixed dried fruits (raisins, currants, apricots)
- 1 1/2 cups regular flour
- 1 pound unsalted butter
- 1 pound brown sugar
- three big eggs
- 1/2 cup plain applesauce
1/4 cup honey 1 teaspoon ground nutmeg
1/2 teaspoon ground cinnamon
1/2 teaspoon baking powder

Preparation:
1. Preheat the oven to 325 degrees Fahrenheit (165 degrees Celsius). Line a 9-inch round cake pan with parchment paper and grease it.
2. Cream the butter and brown sugar together in a large mixing basin until light and fluffy. Beat in the eggs one at a time, beating well after each addition.

3. Combine the flour, nutmeg, cinnamon, and baking powder in a separate basin. Add the dry ingredients to the wet mixture gradually, mixing until just mixed.

4. Stir in the dried fruits, almonds, applesauce, and honey.

5. Smooth the top of the batter into the prepared cake pan.

6. Bake for 2.5 to 3 hours, or until a toothpick inserted into the center of the cake comes out clean. Allow the cake to cool for 30 minutes in the pan before transferring to a wire rack to cool entirely.

**Happy holidays!
Here's wishing you
all the joys of the season
and the happiness
all throughout the upcoming year.**

EVERYDAY**POWER**

6. Fruit and Nut Cake in Winter Wonderland

Ingredients:
- 1 1/2 cup dried fruit mixture (raisins, currants, figs)
- 1 cup chopped mixed nuts (macadamia nuts, Brazil nuts, and pine nuts)
- 1 1/2 cups regular flour
- 1 pound unsalted butter
granulated sugar, 1/2 cup
- three big eggs
- 1/2 cup plain applesauce
1 teaspoon ground cinnamon - 1/4 cup agave nectar
- 1/2 teaspoon ginger powder
1/2 teaspoon baking powder

Preparation:
1. Preheat the oven to 325 degrees Fahrenheit (165 degrees Celsius). Line a 9-inch round cake pan with parchment paper and grease it.
2. Cream the butter and sugar together in a large mixing basin until light and fluffy. Beat in the eggs one at a time, beating well after each addition.

3. Combine the flour, cinnamon, ginger, and baking powder in a separate basin. Add the dry ingredients to the wet mixture gradually, mixing until just mixed.

4. Stir in the dried fruits, almonds, applesauce, and agave nectar.

5. Smooth the top of the batter into the prepared cake pan.

6. Bake for 2.5 to 3 hours, or until a toothpick inserted into the center of the cake comes out clean. Allow the cake to cool for 30 minutes in the pan before transferring to a wire rack to cool entirely.

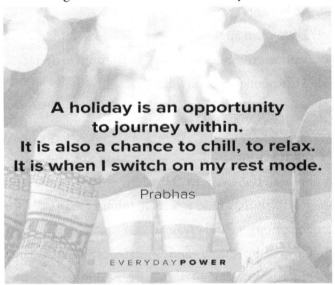

A holiday is an opportunity
to journey within.
It is also a chance to chill, to relax.
It is when I switch on my rest mode.

Prabhas

EVERYDAY**POWER**

Non-alcoholic Fruitcake Muffins

1. Fruit Medley Muffins for the Holidays

Ingredients:
- 1 cup dried fruit mixture (raisins, currants, apricots)
- 1/2 cup mixed nuts (walnuts, almonds, pecans) chopped
- 1 1/2 cups regular flour
- 1 pound unsalted butter
- 1 pound brown sugar
- 2 medium eggs
- 1/2 cup plain applesauce
1/2 teaspoon ground cinnamon
1/4 teaspoon ground nutmeg
1/2 teaspoon baking powder

Preparation:
1. Preheat the oven to 350 degrees Fahrenheit (175 degrees Celsius). Prepare a muffin pan with paper liners.

2. Cream the butter and brown sugar together in a large mixing basin until light and fluffy. Beat in the eggs one at a time, beating well after each addition.

3. Combine the flour, cinnamon, nutmeg, and baking powder in a separate basin. Add the dry ingredients to the wet mixture gradually, mixing until just mixed.

4. Stir in the dried fruits, nuts, and applesauce.

5. Divide the mixture evenly among the muffin cups, filling them approximately two-thirds full.

6. Bake the muffins for 20-25 minutes, or until a toothpick inserted into the center comes out clean. Allow the muffins to rest for a few minutes in the pan before transferring to a wire rack to cool fully.

2. Nutty Orchard Bliss Muffins

Ingredients:
- 1 cup dried fruit mixture (raisins, currants, dates)
- 1/2 cup mixed nuts (cashews, hazelnuts, pistachios) chopped
- 1 1/2 cups regular flour
- 1 pound unsalted butter
- ½ cup of granulated sugar

- 2 medium eggs

- 1/2 cup plain applesauce

1/4 cup honey

1/2 teaspoon powdered cloves

1/4 teaspoon ground cinnamon

1/2 teaspoon baking soda

Preparation:

1. Preheat the oven to 350 degrees Fahrenheit (175 degrees Celsius). Prepare a muffin pan with paper liners.

2. Cream the butter and sugar together in a large mixing basin until light and fluffy. Beat in the eggs one at a time, beating well after each addition.

3. Combine the flour, cloves, cinnamon, and baking soda in a separate basin. Add the dry ingredients to the wet mixture gradually, mixing until just mixed.

4. Stir in the dried fruits, almonds, applesauce, and honey.

5. Divide the mixture evenly among the muffin cups, filling them approximately two-thirds full.

6. Bake the muffins for 20-25 minutes, or until a toothpick inserted into the center comes out clean. Allow the muffins to rest for a few minutes in the pan before transferring to a wire rack to cool fully.

3. Muffins with Orchard Harvest Spice

Ingredients:
- 1 cup dried fruit mixture (raisins, currants, sultanas)
- 1/2 cup mixed nuts (walnuts, almonds, cashews) chopped
- 1 1/2 cups regular flour
- 1 pound unsalted butter
- 1 pound brown sugar
- 2 medium eggs
- 1/2 cup plain applesauce

1/2 teaspoon ground allspice

1/4 teaspoon ground ginger

1/2 teaspoon baking powder

Preparation:
1. Preheat the oven to 350 degrees Fahrenheit (175 degrees Celsius). Prepare a muffin pan with paper liners.
2. Cream the butter and brown sugar together in a large mixing basin until light and fluffy. Beat in the eggs one at a time, beating well after each addition.

3. Combine the flour, allspice, ginger, and baking powder in a separate basin. Add the dry ingredients to the wet mixture gradually, mixing until just mixed.

4. Stir in the dried fruits, nuts, and applesauce.

5. Divide the mixture evenly among the muffin cups, filling them approximately two-thirds full.

6. Bake the muffins for 20-25 minutes, or until a toothpick inserted into the center comes out clean. Allow the muffins to rest for a few minutes in the pan before transferring to a wire rack to cool fully.

4. Holiday Spiced Nut Muffins

Ingredients:

- 1 cup dried fruit mixture (raisins, currants, figs)
- 1/2 cup chopped mixed nuts (macadamia nuts, Brazil nuts, and pine nuts)
- 1 1/2 cups regular flour
- 1 pound unsalted butter
-½ granulated sugar
- 2 medium eggs
- 1/2 cup plain applesauce
- 1 tablespoon maple syrup
1/2 teaspoon ground cinnamon
1/4 teaspoon ground cloves
1/2 teaspoon baking soda

Preparation:

1. Preheat the oven to 350 degrees Fahrenheit (175 degrees Celsius). Prepare a muffin pan with paper liners.
2. Cream the butter and sugar together in a large mixing basin until light and fluffy. Beat in the eggs one at a time, beating well after each addition.

3. Combine the flour, cinnamon, cloves, and baking soda in a separate basin. Add the dry ingredients to the wet mixture gradually, mixing until just mixed.

4. Stir in the dried fruits, almonds, applesauce, and maple syrup.

5. Divide the mixture evenly among the muffin cups, filling them approximately two-thirds full.

6. Bake the muffins for 20-25 minutes, or until a toothpick inserted into the center comes out clean. Allow the muffins to rest for a few minutes in the pan before transferring to a wire rack to cool fully.

Wishing you a fun-filled Holiday season and best wishes for a Happy New Year!

5. Healthy Nut and Spice Muffins

Ingredients:

- 1 cup dried fruit mixture (raisins, currants, dates)
- 1/2 cup mixed nuts (walnuts, almonds, pistachios) chopped
- 1 1/2 cups regular flour
- 1 pound unsalted butter
- 1 pound brown sugar
- 2 medium eggs
- 1/2 cup plain applesauce

1/4 cup honey

1/2 teaspoon ground nutmeg

1/4 teaspoon ground cinnamon

1/2 teaspoon baking powder

Preparation:

1. Preheat the oven to 350 degrees Fahrenheit (175 degrees Celsius). Prepare a muffin pan with paper liners.

2. Cream the butter and brown sugar together in a large mixing basin until light and fluffy. Beat in the eggs one at a time, beating well after each addition.

3. Combine the flour, nutmeg, cinnamon, and baking powder in a separate basin. Add the dry ingredients to the wet mixture gradually, mixing until just mixed.

4. Stir in the dried fruits, almonds, applesauce, and honey.

5. Fill the muffin cups about two-thirds of the way with the batter.

6. Bake the muffins for 20-25 minutes, or until a toothpick inserted into the center comes out clean. Allow the muffins to rest for a few minutes in the pan before transferring to a wire rack to cool fully.

Non-Alcoholic Gluten-Free Fruitcakes

1. Tropical Paradise Gluten-Free Fruitcake

Ingredients:
- 1 cup dried fruit mixture (raisins, currants, apricots)
- 1/2 cup mixed nuts (walnuts, almonds, pecans) chopped
- 1 1/2 cups all-purpose gluten-free flour
- 1 pound unsalted butter
- 1 pound brown sugar
- 2 medium eggs
- 1/2 cup plain applesauce
1/2 teaspoon ground cinnamon
1/4 teaspoon ground nutmeg
- 1 tablespoon gluten-free baking powder

Preparation:

1. Preheat the oven to 350 degrees Fahrenheit (175 degrees Celsius). Using parchment paper, line a 9-inch round cake pan.

2. Cream the butter and brown sugar together in a large mixing basin until light and creamy. Beat in the eggs one at a time, beating well after each addition.

3. Combine the gluten-free flour, cinnamon, nutmeg, and gluten-free baking powder in a separate basin. Add the dry ingredients to the wet mixture gradually, mixing until just mixed.

4. Fold in the dried mixed fruits, almonds, and applesauce.

5. Smooth the top of the batter into the prepared cake pan.

6. 30 minutes, or until a toothpick inserted into the middle comes out clean. Allow the cake to cool for 15 minutes in the pan before transferring to a wire rack to cool entirely.

2. Gluten-Free Fruitcake with Nutty Orchard Bliss

Ingredients:

- 1 cup dried fruit mixture (raisins, currants, dates)
- 1/2 cup mixed nuts (cashews, hazelnuts, pistachios) chopped
- 1 1/2 cups all-purpose gluten-free flour
- 1 pound unsalted butter

½ granulated sugar

- 2 medium eggs
- 1/2 cup plain applesauce
- 1 tablespoon honey

1/2 teaspoon ground cloves

1/4 teaspoon ground cinnamon

- 1/2 teaspoon gluten-free baking powder

Preparation:

1. Preheat the oven to 350 degrees Fahrenheit (175 degrees Celsius). Using parchment paper, line a 9-inch round cake pan.

2. Cream the butter and sugar together in a large mixing basin until light and creamy. Beat in the eggs one at a time, beating well after each addition.

3. Combine the gluten-free flour, cloves, cinnamon, and gluten-free baking soda in a separate basin. Add the dry ingredients to the wet mixture gradually, mixing until just mixed.

4. Mix in the dried fruits, almonds, applesauce, and honey.

5. Smooth the top of the batter into the prepared cake pan.

6. 30 minutes, or until a toothpick inserted into the middle comes out clean. Allow the cake to cool for 15 minutes in the pan before transferring to a wire rack to cool entirely.

3. Gluten-Free Fruit and Nut Cake from Heavenly Harvest

Ingredients:
- 1 cup dried fruit mixture (raisins, currants, apricots)
- 1/2 cup chopped mixed nuts (macadamia nuts, Brazil nuts, and pine nuts)
- 1 1/2 cups all-purpose gluten-free flour
- 1 pound unsalted butter
- 1 pound brown sugar
- 2 medium eggs
- 1/2 cup plain applesauce
- 1 tablespoon agave nectar
- 1/2 teaspoon ginger powder
1/4 teaspoon ground allspice
- 1 tablespoon gluten-free baking powder

Preparation:
1. Preheat the oven to 350 degrees Fahrenheit (175 degrees Celsius). Using parchment paper, line a 9-inch round cake pan.
2. Cream the butter and brown sugar together in a large mixing basin until light and creamy. Beat in the eggs one at a time, beating well after each addition.

3. Combine the gluten-free flour, ginger, allspice, and gluten-free baking powder in a separate basin. Add the dry ingredients to the wet mixture gradually, mixing until just mixed.

4. Mix in the dried fruits, almonds, applesauce, and agave nectar.

5. Smooth the top of the batter into the prepared cake pan.

6. 30 minutes, or until a toothpick inserted into the middle comes out clean. Allow the cake to cool for 15 minutes in the pan before transferring to a wire rack to cool entirely.

4. Gluten Free Loaf of Festive Orchard Nuts and Fruit

Ingredients:

- 1 cup dried fruit mixture (raisins, currants, sultanas)
- 1/2 cup mixed nuts (pecans, almonds, cashews) chopped
- 1 1/2 cups all-purpose gluten-free flour
- 1 pound unsalted butter
½ granulated sugar

- 2 medium eggs
- 1/2 cup plain applesauce
- 1 tablespoon maple syrup
1/2 teaspoon ground cinnamon
1/4 teaspoon ground cloves
- 1 tablespoon gluten-free baking powder

Preparation:

1. Preheat the oven to 350 degrees Fahrenheit (175 degrees Celsius). Using parchment paper, line a 9-inch round cake pan.

2. Cream the butter and sugar together in a large mixing basin until light and creamy. Beat in the eggs one at a time, beating well after each addition.

3. Combine the gluten-free flour, cinnamon, cloves, and gluten-free baking powder in a separate basin. Add the dry ingredients to the wet mixture gradually, mixing until just mixed.

4. Mix in the dried fruits, almonds, applesauce, and maple syrup.

5. Smooth the top of the batter into the prepared cake pan.

6. 30 minutes, or until a toothpick inserted into the middle comes out clean. Allow the cake to cool for 15 minutes in the pan before transferring to a wire rack to cool entirely.

5. Gluten Free Delicious Nut and Fruit Medley Cake

Ingredients:
- 1 cup dried fruit mixture (raisins, currants, dates)
- 1/2 cup mixed nuts (walnuts, almonds, pistachios) chopped
- 1 1/2 cups all-purpose gluten-free flour
- 1 pound unsalted butter
- 1 pound brown sugar

- 2 medium eggs
- 1/2 cup plain applesauce
- 1 tablespoon honey

1/2 teaspoon ground nutmeg
- 1/4 teaspoon ground cinnamon
- 1 tablespoon gluten-free baking powder

Preparation:

1. Preheat the oven to 350 degrees Fahrenheit (175 degrees Celsius). Using parchment paper, line a 9-inch round cake pan.

2. Cream the butter and brown sugar together in a large mixing basin until light and creamy. Beat in the eggs one at a time, beating well after each addition.

3. Combine the gluten-free flour, nutmeg, cinnamon, and gluten-free baking powder in a separate basin. Add the dry ingredients to the wet mixture gradually, mixing until just mixed.

4. Mix in the dried fruits, almonds, applesauce, and honey.

5. Smooth the top of the batter into the prepared cake pan.

6. 30 minutes, or until a toothpick inserted into the middle comes out clean. Allow the cake to cool for 15 minutes in the pan before transferring to a wire rack to cool entirely.

Merry everything and a happy always.

Chapter 3

Non-Alcoholic Fruitcake Decorating and Presentation Ideas

Fruitcakes have a long history as a popular delicacy, particularly during the Christmas season. Presentation is essential when baking a non-alcoholic fruitcake for a special event or as a pleasant gift for friends and family. A tastefully decorated fruit cake not only looks appealing but also demonstrates the care and attention that went into its production. In this article, we'll look at several ways to decorate and serve non-alcoholic fruitcakes to make them more attractive.

Decorating and presenting a non-alcoholic fruitcake is an art form that can elevate a simple dessert to a work of beauty. It's an opportunity to express yourself by personalizing the fruitcake and make it the focal point of your party. In this section, we'll go over the essentials for having your non-alcoholic fruitcake look as delicious as it tastes.

1. Select the Best Fruitcake Recipe

Before you begin embellishing, you must first prepare a delectable base. Select a non-alcoholic fruitcake recipe that suits your taste and dietary needs. The flavor and texture of your cake are the foundation of the ornamentation, whether you like a traditional fruitcake or a modern touch.

2. Begin by creating a smooth icing base.

Icing serves as a blank canvas for your creations. A coating of icing that is smooth and even will serve as the perfect backdrop for your creative touches. Cream cheese frosting, marzipan, or a conventional royal icing are common alternatives for non-alcoholic fruitcakes. Make sure the frosting is properly distributed and free of lumps or air bubbles.

3. Utilize Royal Icing

Royal icing is a traditional method for adorning fruitcakes. It dries to a firm, smooth sheen and makes an excellent background for detailed drawings. Combine egg whites or meringue powder, powdered sugar, and a splash of lemon juice to make royal icing. Add water or powdered sugar to adjust the consistency till it's simple to pipe and distribute. Royal icing may be tinted using food coloring gels to provide a variety of hues for your embellishments.

4. Select Your Color Scheme

Consider the color palette that suits your event or theme when arranging your fruitcake decorating. Traditional Christmas hues like green, red, and white work nicely, while pastel tints are ideal for spring and Easter. Keep in mind that the color of your frosting and decorations may help to create the tone and atmosphere for your presentation.

5. Borders with ornamentation

A stylish border around your non-alcoholic fruitcake provides a professional touch. Piped pearls, shells, or scalloped edges with a piping bag are simple yet lovely possibilities. You may also use fondant or marzipan to make beautiful borders around the cake, such as braids or ropes.

6. Flowers and Leaves that are edible

Edible flowers and foliage may add a natural touch to your fruitcake. Candied violets, pansies, or rose petals offer a splash of color and sophistication. If you're talented with sugarcraft, you may make edible flowers out of gum paste or fondant to decorate your cake.

7. Messages That Are Unique

Including a handwritten note or welcome on your fruitcake is a lovely way to gift it. You may write directly on the cake's surface using edible markers or make a fondant or marzipan plaque with your message. This is an excellent method to express best wishes or commemorate memorable events.

8. The Piping Technique

Piping is a flexible method for creating complicated shapes with accuracy. Purchase a set of pipe tips and experiment with different patterns and shapes. With royal icing, you may create ornamental borders, flower patterns, and even delicate lace motifs. For consistent results, keep a steady hand and manage the pressure on the piping bag.

9. Think about Texture.

The addition of texture to your non-alcoholic fruitcake may provide depth and appeal. Texture can be added using techniques like stenciling, brush embroidery, or a textured impression mat. These techniques may give your cake a distinct and tactile touch.

10. gilded opulence

Consider using edible gold or silver leaf for a sense of elegance. Gilding your fruitcake gives a luxurious and eye-catching touch. Edible metallic leaf can be put to icing to create a dazzling, shiny surface.

11. Make use of fresh fruits.

Fresh fruits, such as berries, lemon pieces, or grapes, may help your fruitcake seem more appealing. Arrange them artistically around or on top of the cake. Fresh fruits' brilliant colors and natural textures give a refreshing counterpoint to the cake's richness.

12. Dragees and Nuts

Nuts and dragees (sugar-coated sweets) are excellent ways to add crunch and texture to your fruitcake. For a beautiful touch, consider adding whole or chopped nuts along the borders or using dragees as edible pearls.

13. Include Layers

Layering your non-alcoholic fruitcake might make for a visually stunning display. Begin with a foundation layer of icing, followed by another layer or tiers, and finally, embellish each layer differently. This method may make your cake appear huge and spectacular.

14. Maintain Balance

It is critical to have equilibrium in your decorating. Avoid overcrowding the cake with too many features, which might result in a crowded appearance. Concentrate on a few key design elements and highlight them with simpler accents.

15. Choose Seasonal Décor

Consider using seasonal decorations if you're serving your non-alcoholic fruitcake during a certain season or festival. For example, for Christmas, holly branches and berries, or for Easter, beautiful Easter eggs. Seasonal décor not only looks festive, but it also links your dessert to the season.

16. Include Traditional Symbols

Traditional symbols and motifs can evoke nostalgia and a feeling of tradition. Include symbols such as snowflakes, candy canes, and mistletoe for Christmas. Consider wedding bells or flowers for weddings. These symbols might help to improve the concept of your event.

17. Ribbons can be used to embellish.

Using beautiful ribbons to improve the presentation of your non-alcoholic fruitcake is a simple yet effective method to do so. Wrap a ribbon around the cake's base or make a ribbon bow on top. The ribbon's color and style might complement your overall design.

18. Serve with Class

The presentation of your non-alcoholic fruitcake is also affected by how it is served. Make the cake a prominent point by elevating it with a cake stand or pedestal. For an extra wow factor, serve it with complimentary sweets or a dollop of handmade ice cream.

19. Monograms can be used to add a personal touch.

Monograms or initials made of fondant or marzipan can be used to customize your non-alcoholic fruitcake. Weddings and anniversaries are especially popular occasions for monograms.

20. Display Your Ingenuity

Don't be scared to let your imagination go wild. Fruitcake decorating is an art form with no set restrictions. Try out different techniques, colors, and patterns. Your personal touch will elevate your non-alcoholic fruitcake to a work of art.

21. Exercise, Exercise, Exercise

Fruitcake decorating, like any culinary craft, needs practice. Don't give up if your initial tries aren't ideal. Continue to honeing your talents, and you'll become more adept and confident in your decorating abilities over time.

Decorating and presenting a non-alcoholic fruitcake is a fun project that allows you to express your creativity while also adding a personal touch to your dessert. These methods can help you convert your fruitcake into a visually gorgeous masterpiece, whether you're commemorating a special event, a holiday, or simply indulging in a sweet treat. For the best effects, use the proper color palette, include different textures, and balance your decorations. Your non-alcoholic fruitcake will be the highlight of any celebration with a little skill and flair. Enjoy the procedure and the tasty results of your efforts!

Conclusion

"The Fruitcake Recipe Cookbook" is a fascinating voyage into the world of fruitcakes, with a wide range of recipes to suit every taste and occasion. This detailed tutorial will walk you through the process of making non-alcoholic fruitcakes, including a variety of tastes, materials, and techniques.

You've uncovered a treasure mine of possibilities to fit your preferences, ranging from classic recipes that invoke nostalgic holiday traditions to modern tweaks that add a fresh perspective to this popular dessert. The book has supplied you with step-by-step directions, ingredient lists, and recommendations to guarantee that you always make the ideal fruitcake.

You've also studied the art of decorating and presenting non-alcoholic fruitcakes, discovering how to transform these exquisite delicacies into beautiful masterpieces that delight the sight as well as the tongue. You can now take your fruitcakes to the next level with a variety of unique ideas and techniques, making them the highlight of any event.

Whether you're a seasoned baker or a newbie in the kitchen, this book will provide you with the information and inspiration you need to make fruitcakes that are not only tasty but also a source of joy and happiness for you and those you enjoy them with. Fruitcakes' flexibility allows them to be enjoyed all year round, from special occasions to ordinary pleasures.

Remember that the most important factors for preparing fruitcakes are passion and patience. Experiment, modify, and have fun while making these scrumptious sweets. Fruitcakes have a long history and tradition, and this book has given you the skills to carry on the tradition while putting your own spin.

So, whether you're baking fruitcakes for a special occasion, a cheerful celebration, or just for fun, "The Fruitcake Recipe Cookbook" is your go-to resource. With your newfound knowledge, creativity, and recipes, you're now ready to inject your own magic into each fruitcake, transforming it from a dessert into a symbol of love, warmth, and joy. Happy baking, and may your fruitcakes bring you joy and the joy of people you share them with.

Made in the USA
Monee, IL
11 January 2024

50520575R00066